SUSAN BOYLE
THE GIFT

Produced by
Alfred Music Publishing Co., Inc.
P.O. Box 10003
Van Nuys, CA 91410-0003
alfred.com

Printed in USA.

ISBN-10: 0-7390-7785-6
ISBN-13: 978-0-7390-7785-6

Susan Boyle Photography: Jason Bell
Background image: © iStockphoto.com / Ryan Lane

 Contents printed on recycled paper.

*W*hen making this album, I really wanted the songs to touch hearts. Music has always been a companion to me, particularly on special occasions. Songs can sometimes have a very literal meaning, sometimes they can be open to interpretation. I wanted to tell you a little about what these songs mean to me. I hope you find your own meaning within them also.

✳ PERFECT DAY ✳ 4

We each have a different idea of what our Perfect Day would be and so this Lou Reed song will mean something different to each of us. There have been so many versions of this song, about an idyllic day when everything goes right for you and you and your partner have a peaceful and harmonious time away from the pressures of life. It is also about being responsible, "you will reap what you sow". Relationships are of all different types and all are about this responsibility.

✳ HALLELUJAH ✳ 10

Hallelujah is quite an abstract inclusion in this collection of seasonal songs. It's loosely based on the biblical story of Samson and Delilah. The lure of good over evil. The bittersweetness of revenge. The rebirth of relationships. The power of God over man. This is an unusual one for Christmas, quite a macabre song in some respects, dark. It's totally different to what you would expect a Christmas song to be but it's very powerful, very poignant.

✳ DO YOU HEAR WHAT I HEAR? ✳ 44

Do You Hear What I Hear? is my duet with my Susan Search winner, Amber. We had such fun. This song, about the nativity is a song that involves children, families, everyone, so it was relevant that I sang this with someone. It's very much a feel good song, once again evoking that magic of Christmas.

✳ DON'T DREAM IT'S OVER ✳ 14

Not all the songs on this album are Christmas songs. I wanted there to be a mix that would flow with all our moods during this season. As much as the season is a time for reflection, it is also a time for fun and enjoyment. My version of the Crowded House song Don't Dream It's Over is there to put people in a party mood! It's a real feel good song, a happy tune. It's a very pretty song.

✳ THE FIRST NOEL ✳ 28

The wonderful thing about this season is that it takes us across a range of our emotions and asks us to think deeply as adults but also to cast our minds back to the simple joyfulness of childhood when the magic of Christmas was most meaningful. The First Noel was chosen for the album because it is a Christmas story. Every kid likes to hear a Christmas story and this traditional song tells the story of the Shepherd's journey and the pursuit of a star. It really does bring the magic of Christmas to my mind.

✳ O HOLY NIGHT ✳ 20

O Holy Night recalls a most special night when The King of Kings was born, the real meaning of Christmas. This song captures the essence of what Christmas is all about, capturing the more spiritual aspect of Christmas, celebrating the birth of Christ.

✳ AWAY IN A MANGER ✳ 33

Away In A Manger is about innocence and the fact that God was made man that Christmas Eve. He was born humble with no riches, in a lowly stable. It's a lovely sentiment, humility, something we can all be reminded of. Hearing a particular song can take you back to such graphic memories of the past. I couldn't sing this in the studio without being reminded of The Nativity plays we used to do at school. I was in a couple of nativity plays and there were quite a few fights between the shepherds and the three wise men! So Away In A Manger is a way of recalling those days. It is also about the magic of Christmas for me.

✳ MAKE ME A CHANNEL OF YOUR PEACE ✳ 36

Make Me a Channel Of Your Peace is a well known hymn, very traditional, very beautiful. It's about not being involved in the violence of today, not being involved in political argument and trying to make peace between God and man. My feelings on this can be summed up so simply. Lord use me as your instrument. Let me continue to make people happy. You meant me to do this.

✳ AULD LANG SYNE ✳ 24

Auld Lang Syne is very traditional. It originates from the Burns poem and is exactly what it says – the renewing of resolutions, the passing of the old year to the new. It's such an emotive song, sung by so many people across the world. No matter what your faith or culture, we all have a time of the year when we ask ourselves to make resolutions, and ask whether we have kept those we made before.

✳ O COME ALL YE FAITHFUL ✳ 41

The real magic of Christmas and indeed the whole holiday season is people coming together and this is evoked wonderfully with O Come All Ye Faithful. On one hand is the coming together of everyone to celebrate the birth of Jesus and on the other it is about the coming together of voices to celebrate Christmas. For me it conjures up choirs and carol concerts. You hear O Come All Ye Faithful in the shops, you hear it when choirs practice for carol concerts. So you know Christmas is coming when you hear it for the very first time in the year. Very joyful.

I do hope you enjoy this collection of songs as much as I enjoyed singing them. Wherever you are, and whoever you are with. I hope you have a very happy Christmas and a peaceful and joyful New Year.

With love,

Susan Boyle

November 2010

PERFECT DAY

Words and Music by
LOU REED

HALLELUJAH

Words and Music by
LEONARD COHEN

lu - jah, hal - le - lu - jah.

2. Well, your

jah.

Verse 3:

3. Ba - by, I've been here be - fore, I've

seen this room and I've walked this floor. I used to live a - lone be - fore I

DON'T DREAM IT'S OVER

Words and Music by
NEIL FINN

Verse 2:

You know___ they won't___ win.

2. Now I'm tow - ing my car.___ There's a hole in the roof.___

My pos - ses-sions are caus - ing me sus - pi - cion, but there's___ no proof.___

In the pa - per to - day,___ tales of war and of waste,___

O HOLY NIGHT

Traditional
Arranged by STEVE MAC
and DAVE ARCH

Slowly, with expression ♩. = 52

Verse 1:

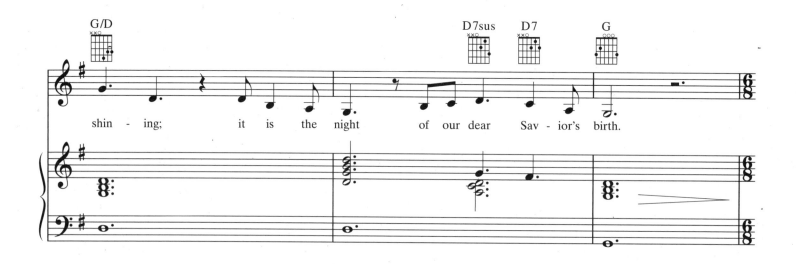

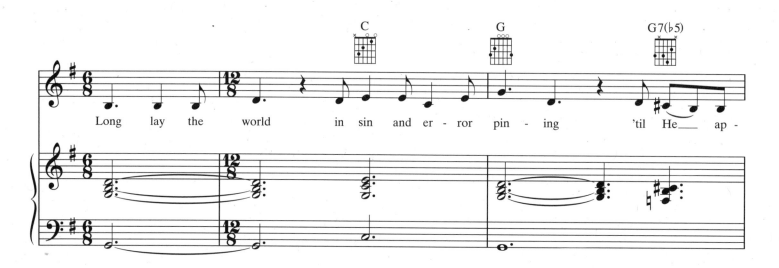

O Holy Night - 4 - 1

AULD LANG SYNE

Traditional
*Arranged by STEVE MAC
and DAVE ARCH*

Chorus:

For Auld_____ Lang____ Syne,   my dear,_   for Auld_

Lang____ Syne.____   We'll take   a   cup__ of   kind -

ness yet   for__ Auld_____ Lang_____ Syne.____

3. Should

THE FIRST NOEL

Traditional
Arranged by STEVE MAC and DAVE ARCH

Verse 2:

32

AWAY IN A MANGER

Traditional
Arranged by STEVE MAC
and DAVE ARCH

MAKE ME A CHANNEL OF YOUR PEACE

Arranged by
SEBASTIAN TEMPLE

Moderately slow ♩ = 80

(with pedal)

A little slower, freely ♩ = 69
Verse 1:

1. Make me a chan-nel of Your peace. Where there is ha-tred, let me bring Your

love. Where this is in-ju-ry, Your par-don, Lord, and

Make Me a Channel of Your Peace - 5 - 1

O COME ALL YE FAITHFUL

Traditional
*Arranged by STEVE MAC
and DAVE ARCH*

Moderately, with expression ♩ = 96

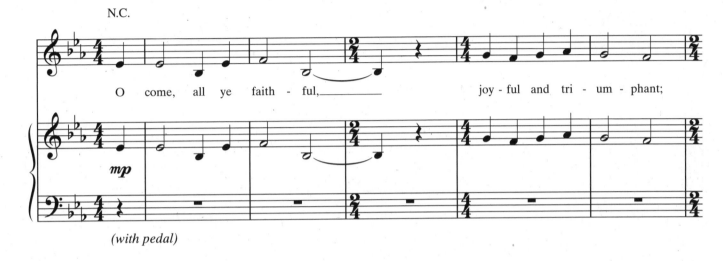

N.C.

O come, all ye faith - ful,_____ joy - ful and tri - um - phant;

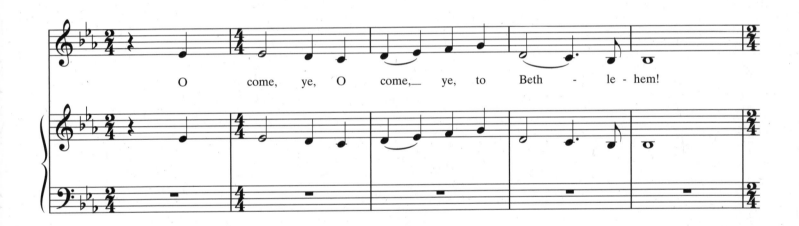

O come, ye, O come,_ ye, to Beth - le - hem!

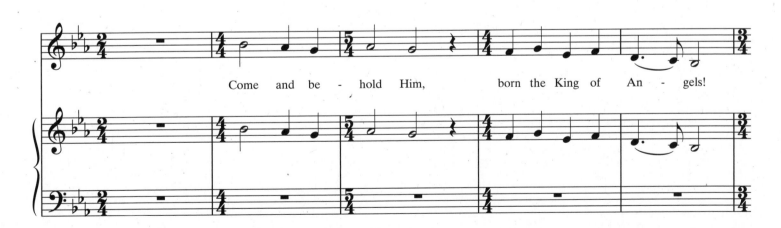

Come and be - hold Him, born the King of An - gels!

O Come All Ye Faithful - 3 - 1

42

O come, let us a - dore Him! O come, let us a - dore Him! O

come, let us a - dore Him,___ Christ___ the Lord!

Sing, choir of an - gels, sing in ex - ul - ta - tion;

Sing all ye cit - i - zens of heav'n___ a - bove.

F/C Gm/C F/C B♭ A7sus A7/C♯

Dm7 C G7 C Dm7(♭5)/A♭ C/E C/G G7 C C/B♭

O Come All Ye Faithful - 3 - 2

DO YOU HEAR WHAT I HEAR?

Words and Music by
NOEL REGNEY and GLORIA SHAYNE

Slowly, very legato throughout ♩ = 69

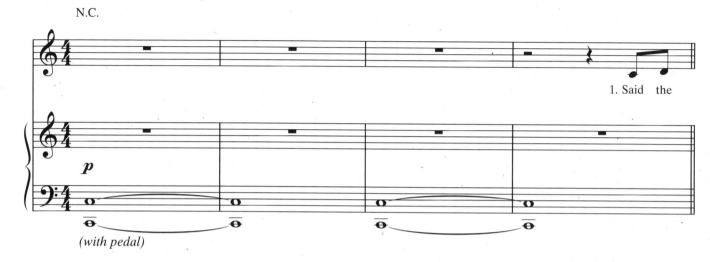

46

Do You Hear What I Hear? - 5 - 3

Verse 3:

shep-herd boy to the might - y king, "Do you know what I know?___

___ In your pal - ace warm, might - y king,___

do you know what I know?___ A child, a child___

shiv - ers___ in the cold, let us bring him sil - ver and gold,___ let us